HELLO SPRING

COLORING BOOK FOR KIDS

THIS BOOK BELONGS TO

_____

Copyright © 2023 Hafida Ben Books
All Right Reserved.

All rights reserved. No part of this publication may be reproduced or used in any form or by any means graphic, electronic, or mechanical, including photocopying, recording, or information storage-and-retrieval without permission of the publisher.

Hello Spring

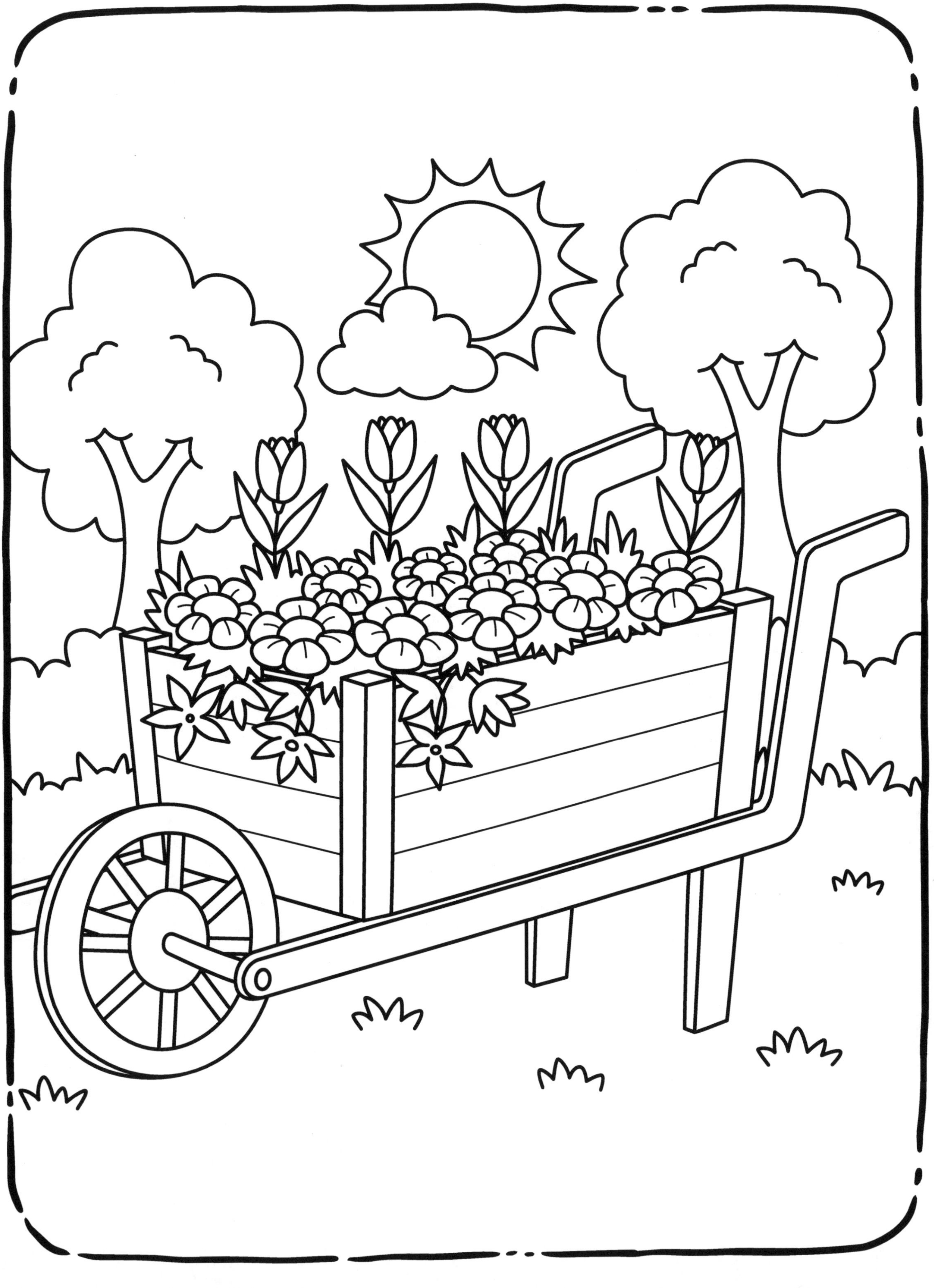

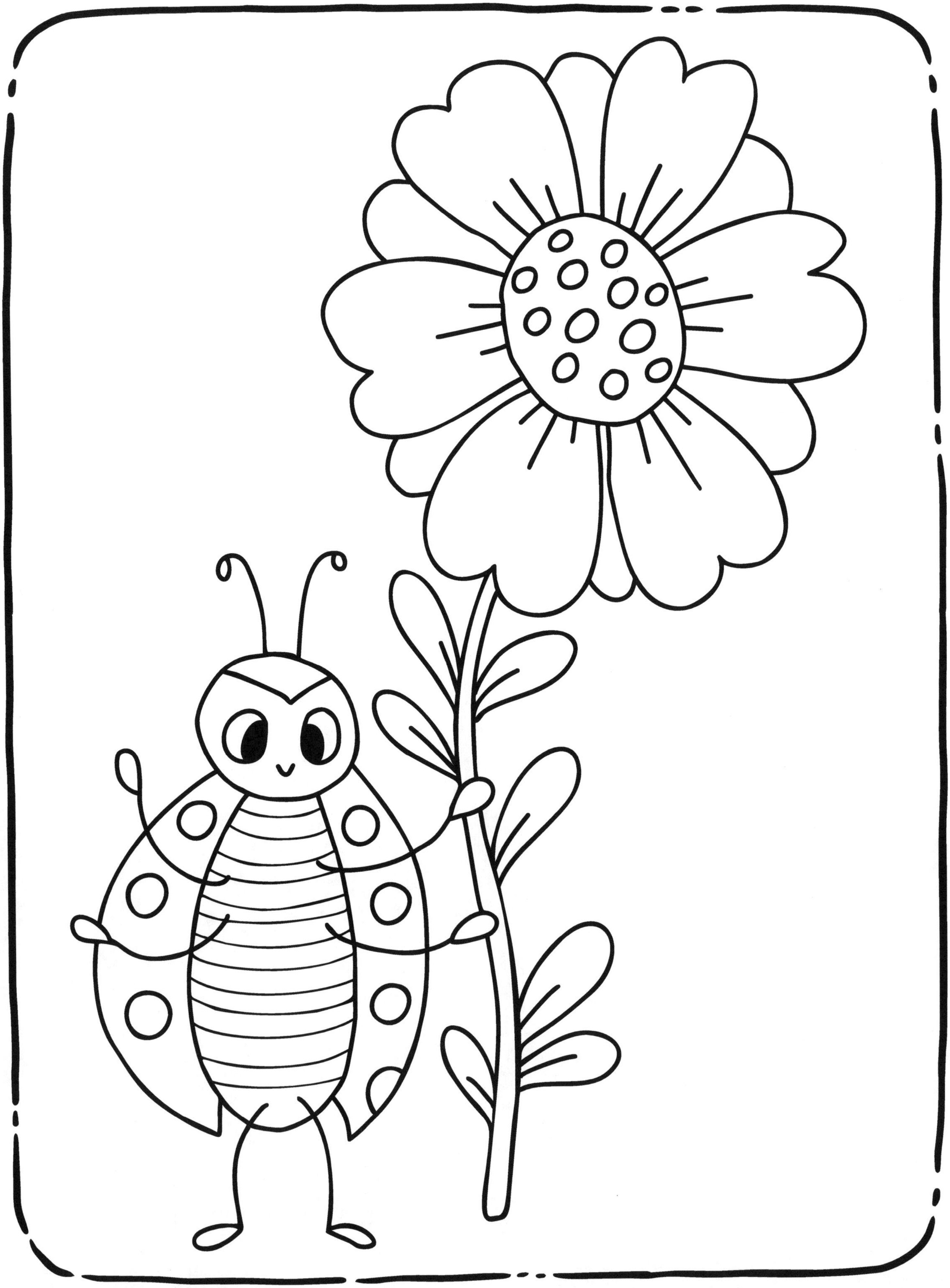

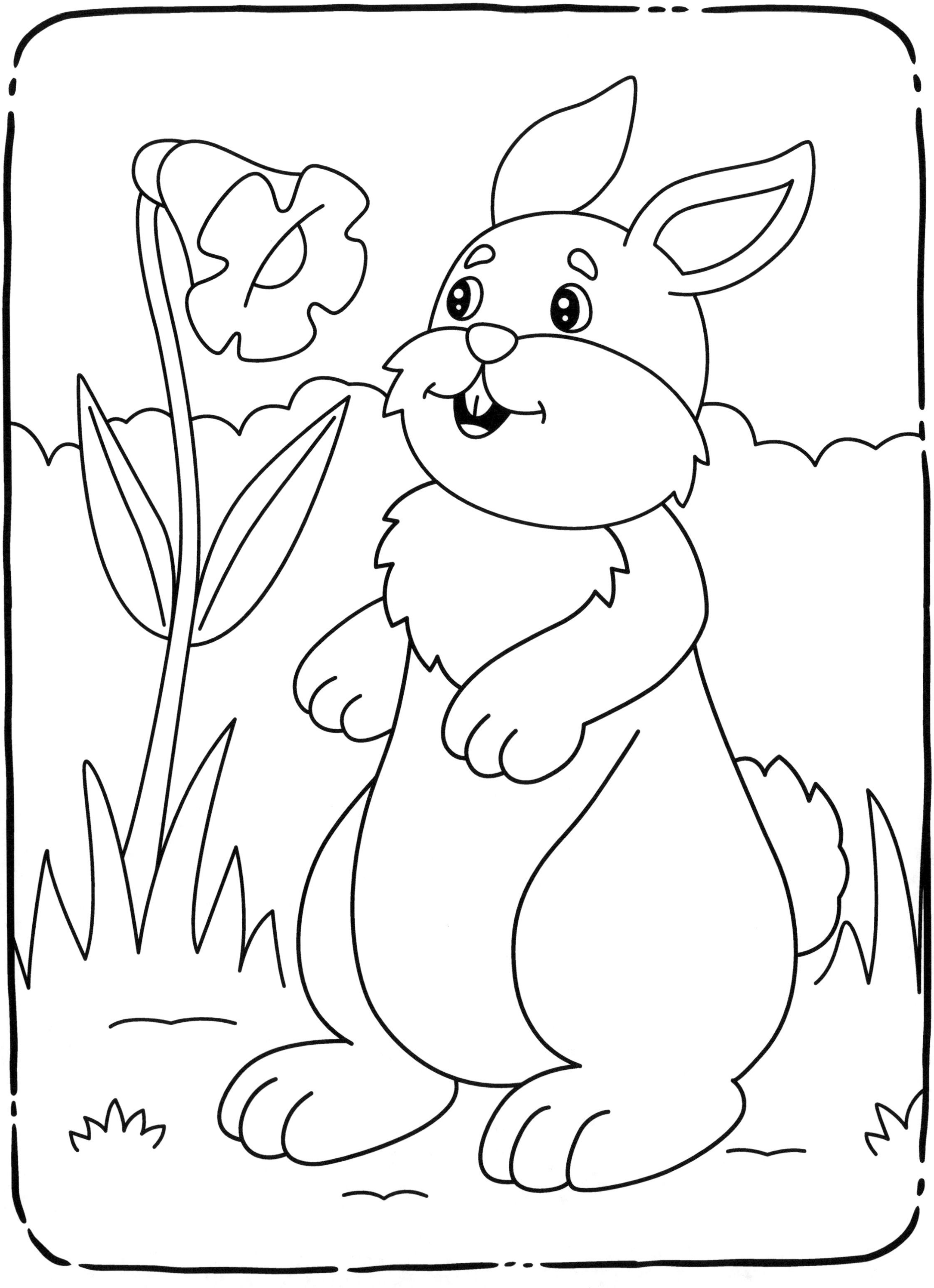

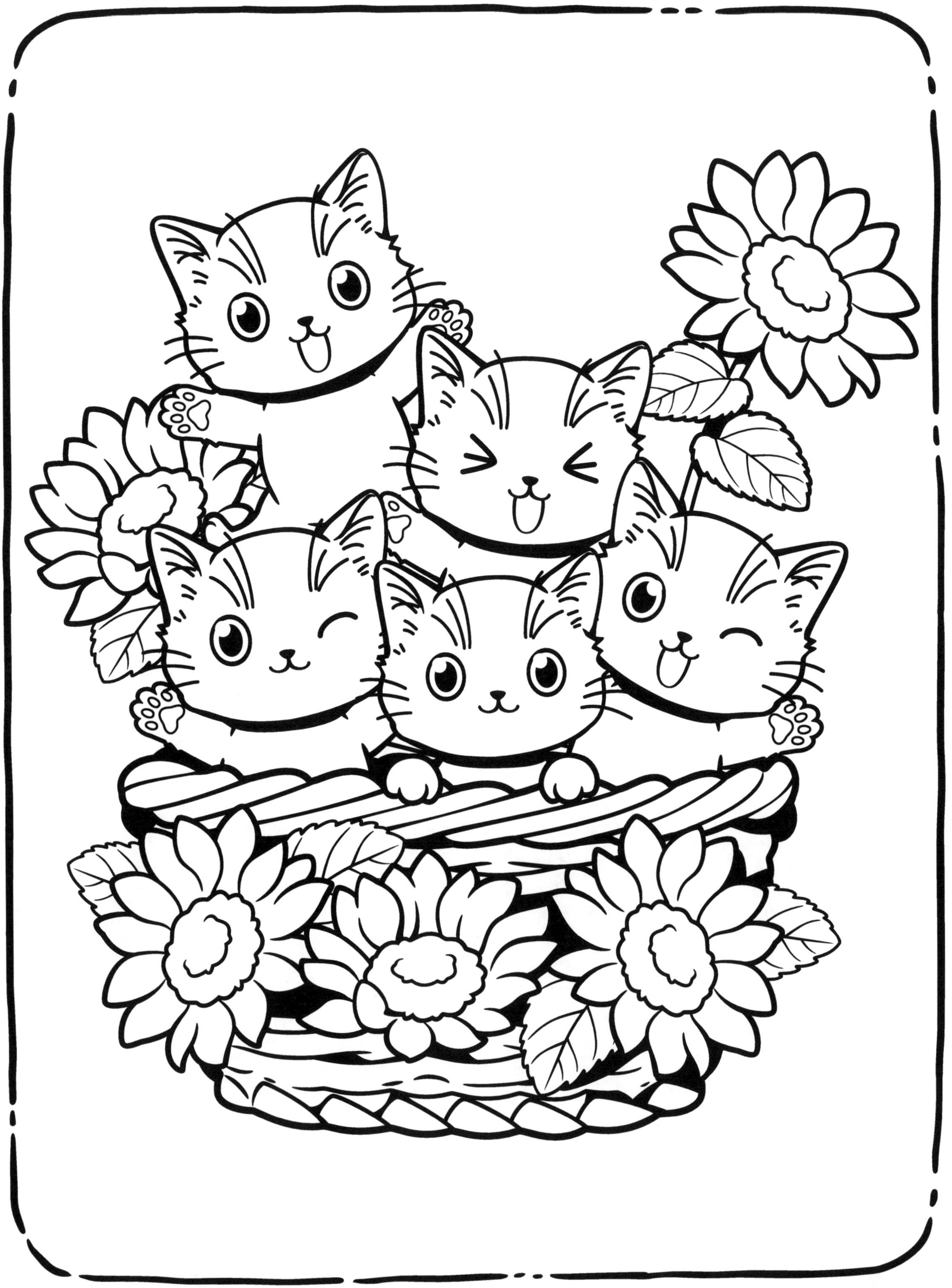

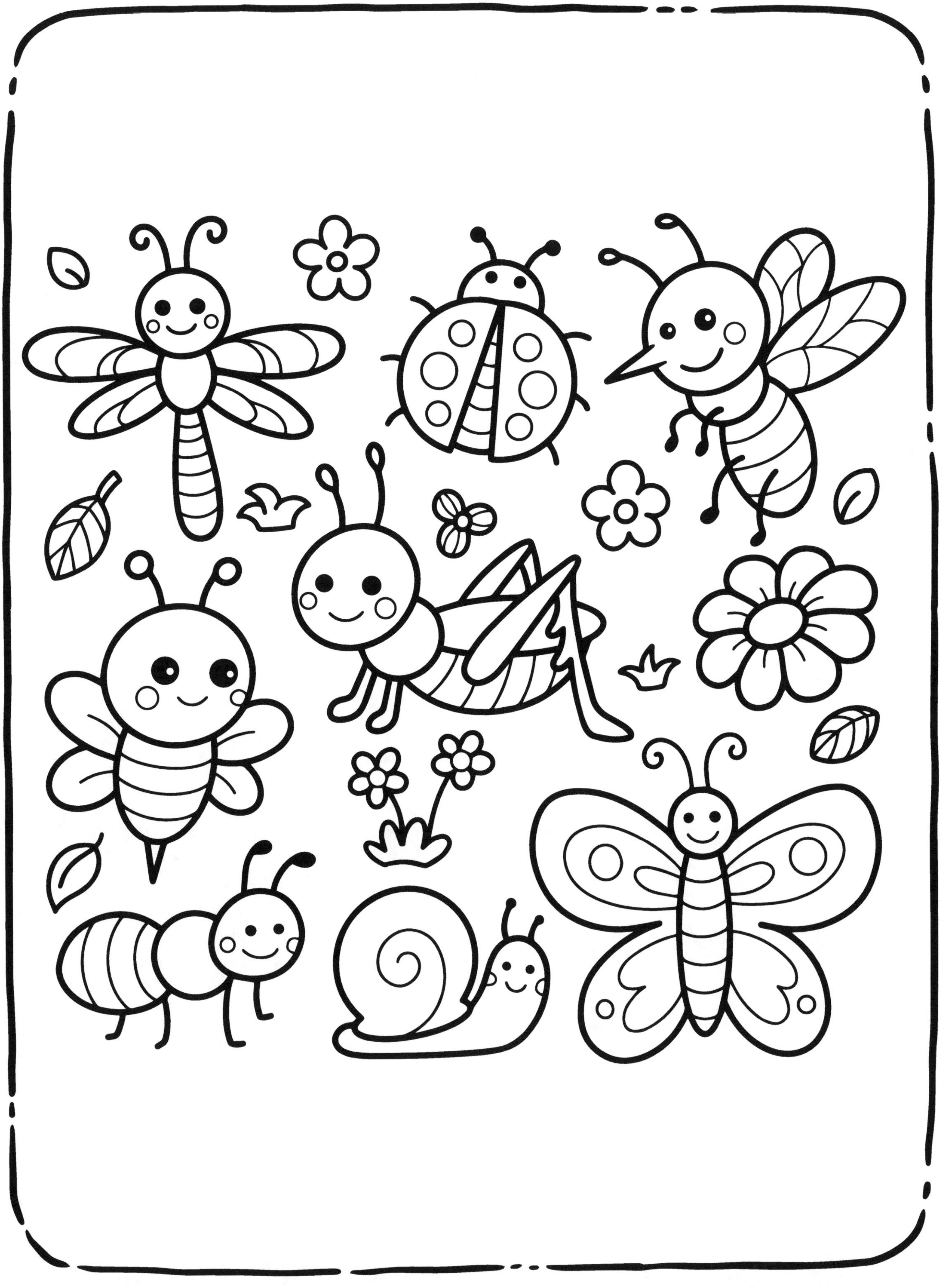

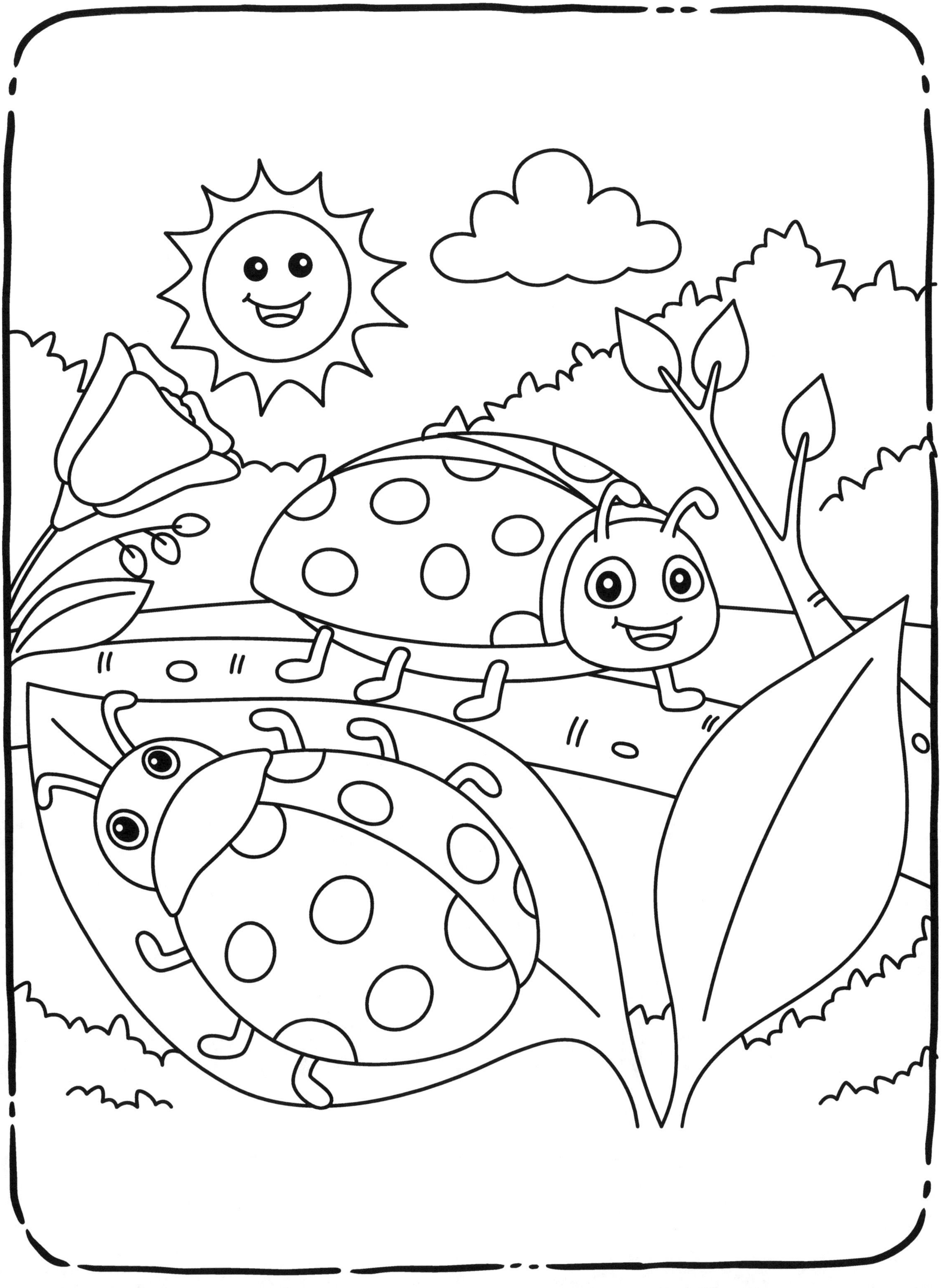

HAPPY SPRING

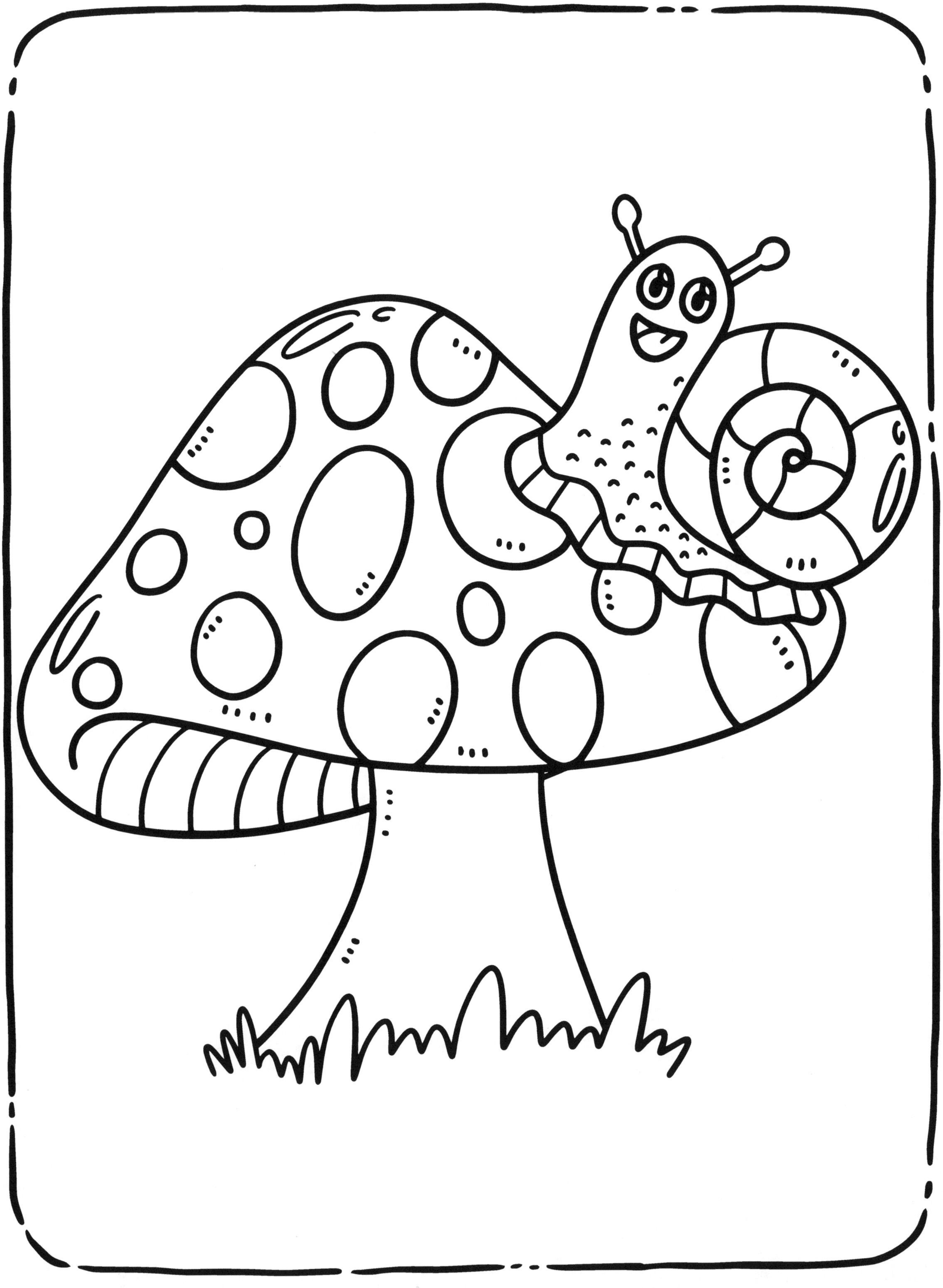

SPRING

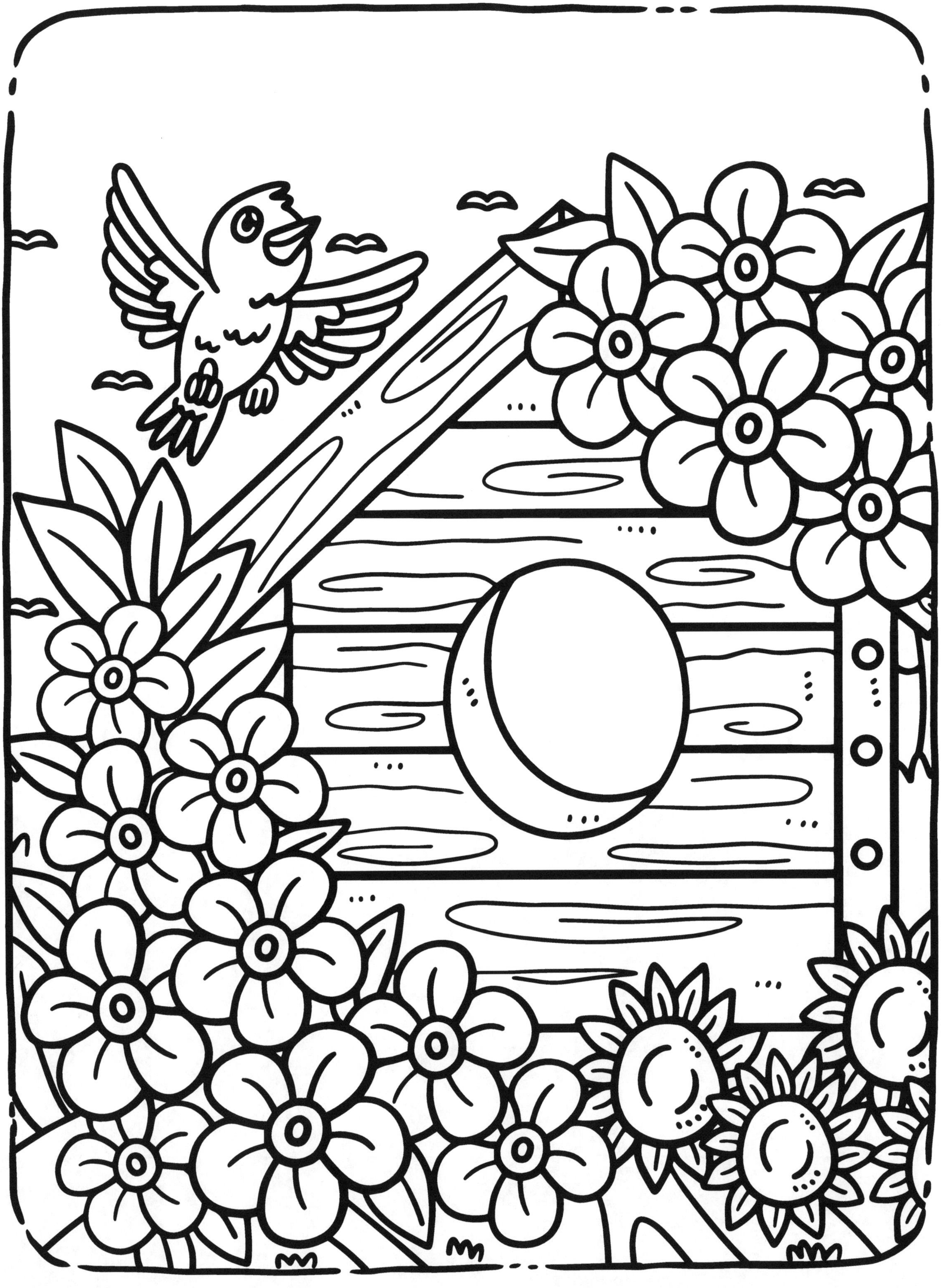

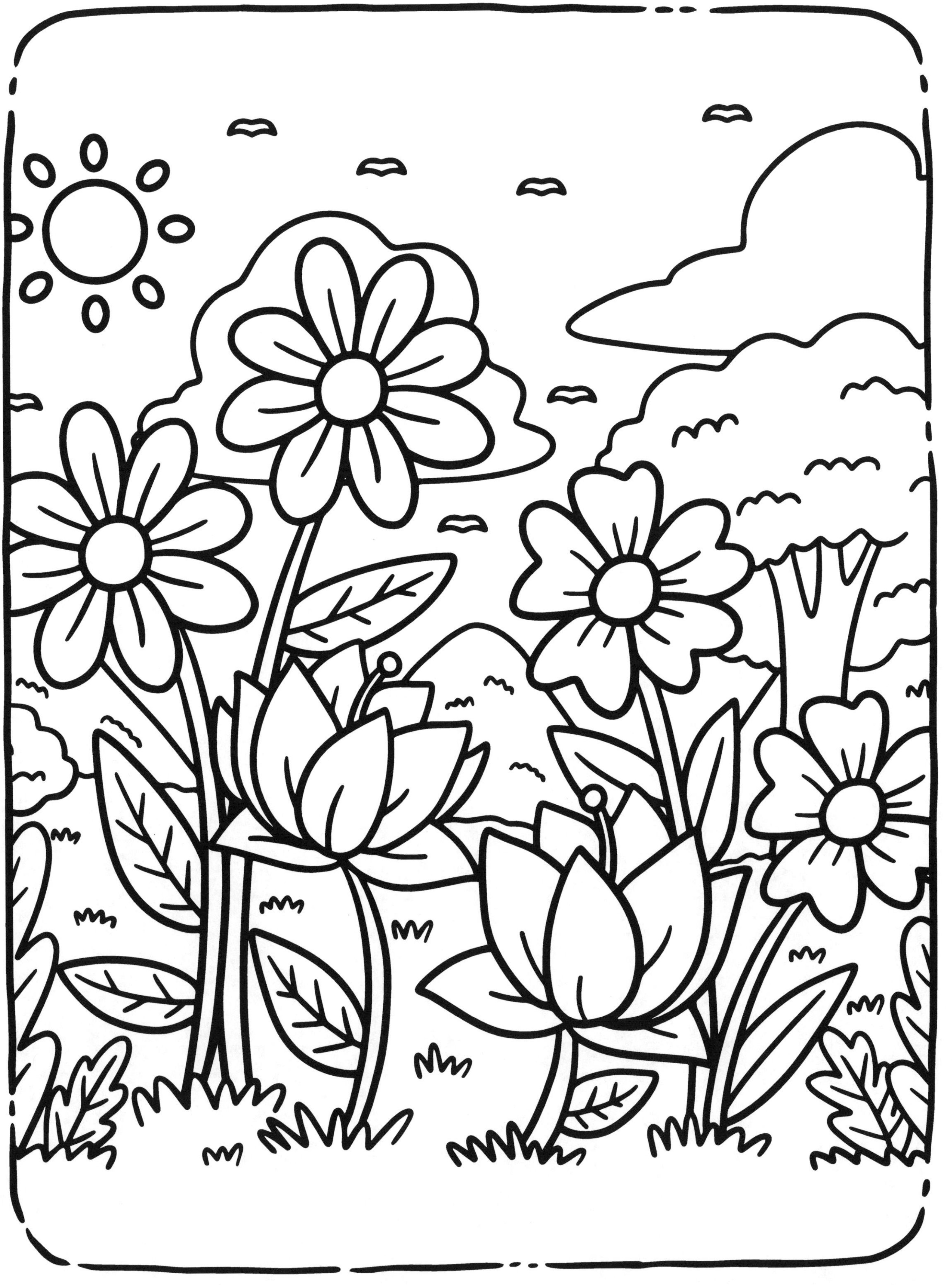

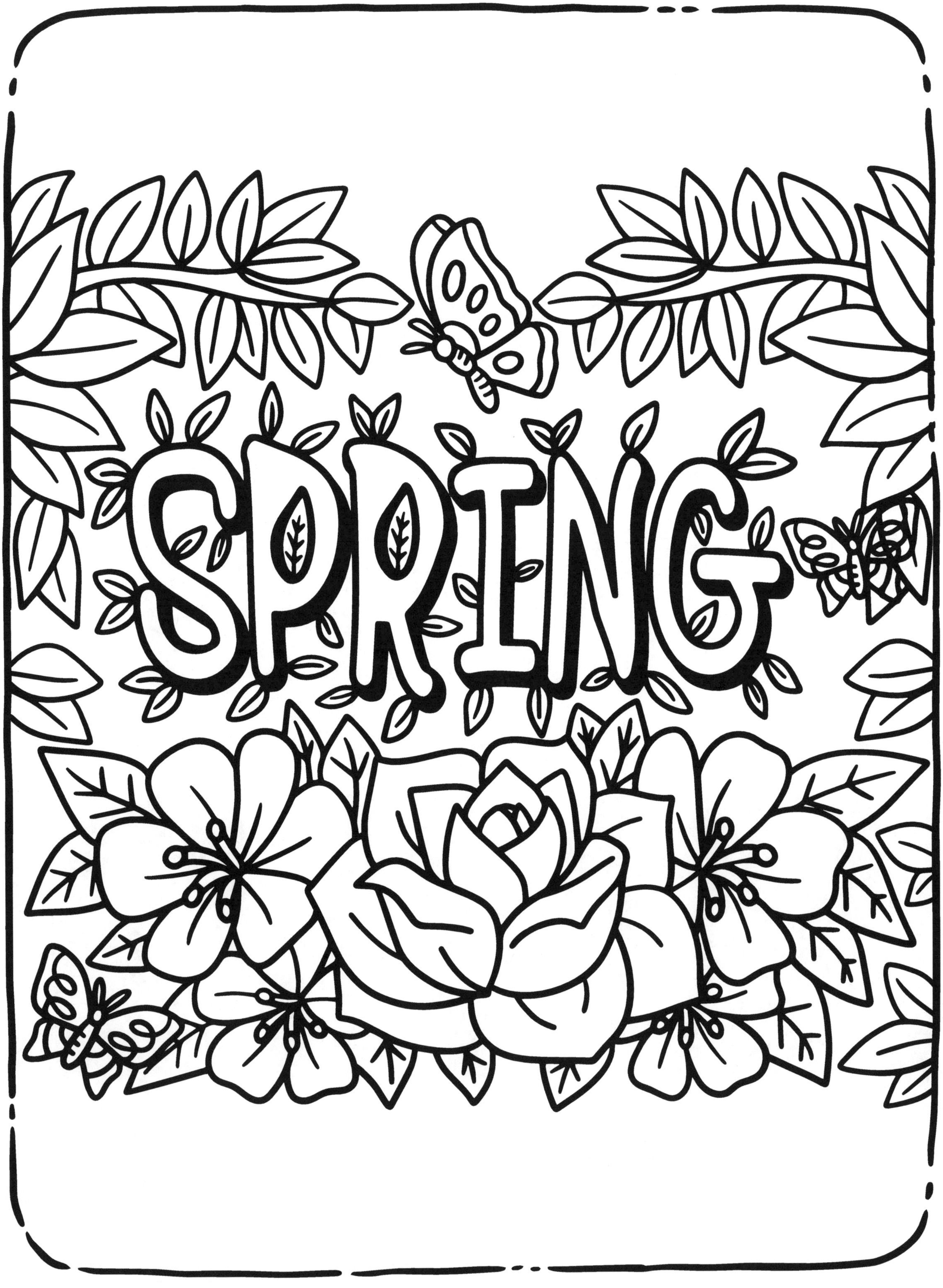
SPRING

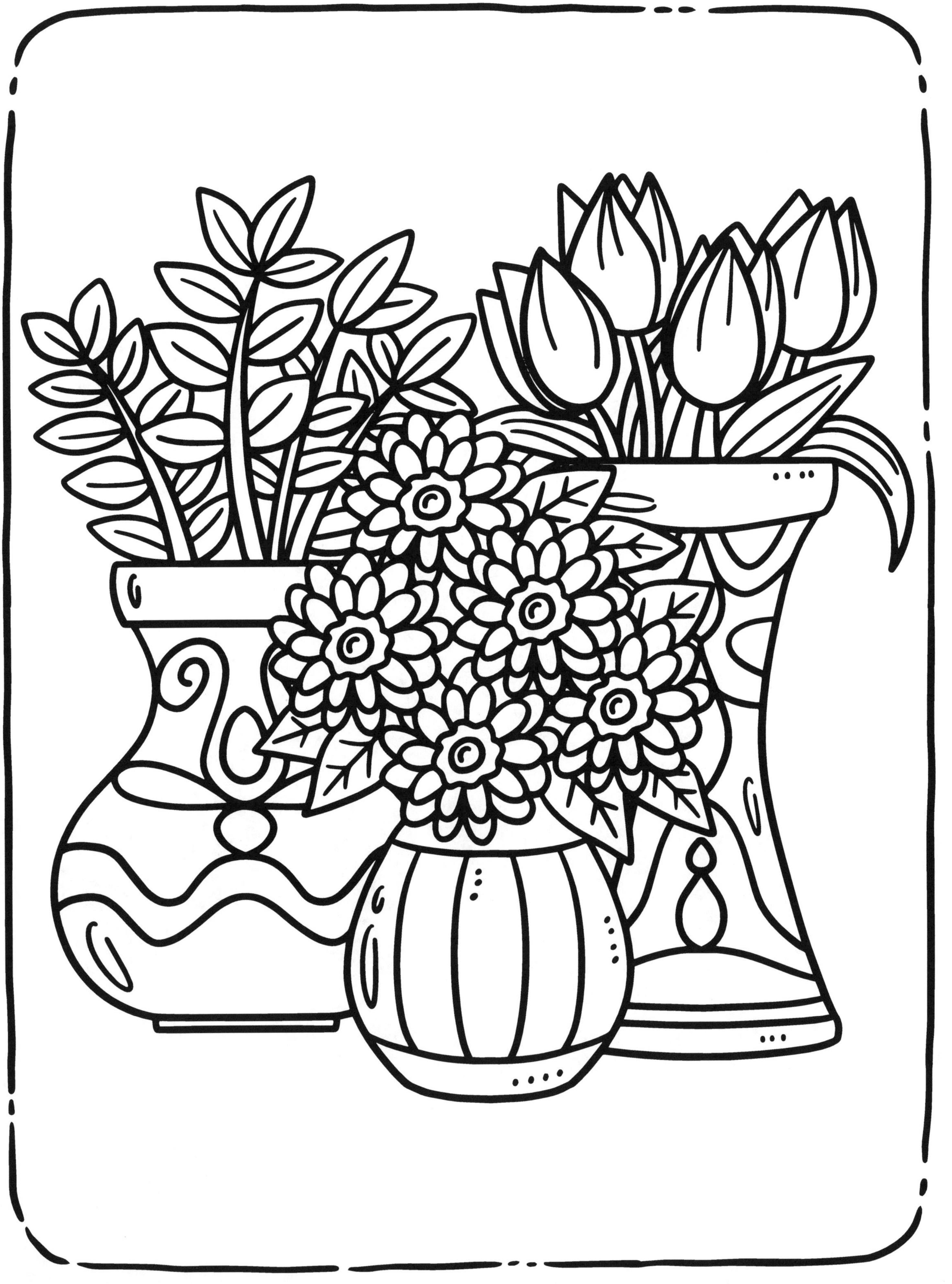

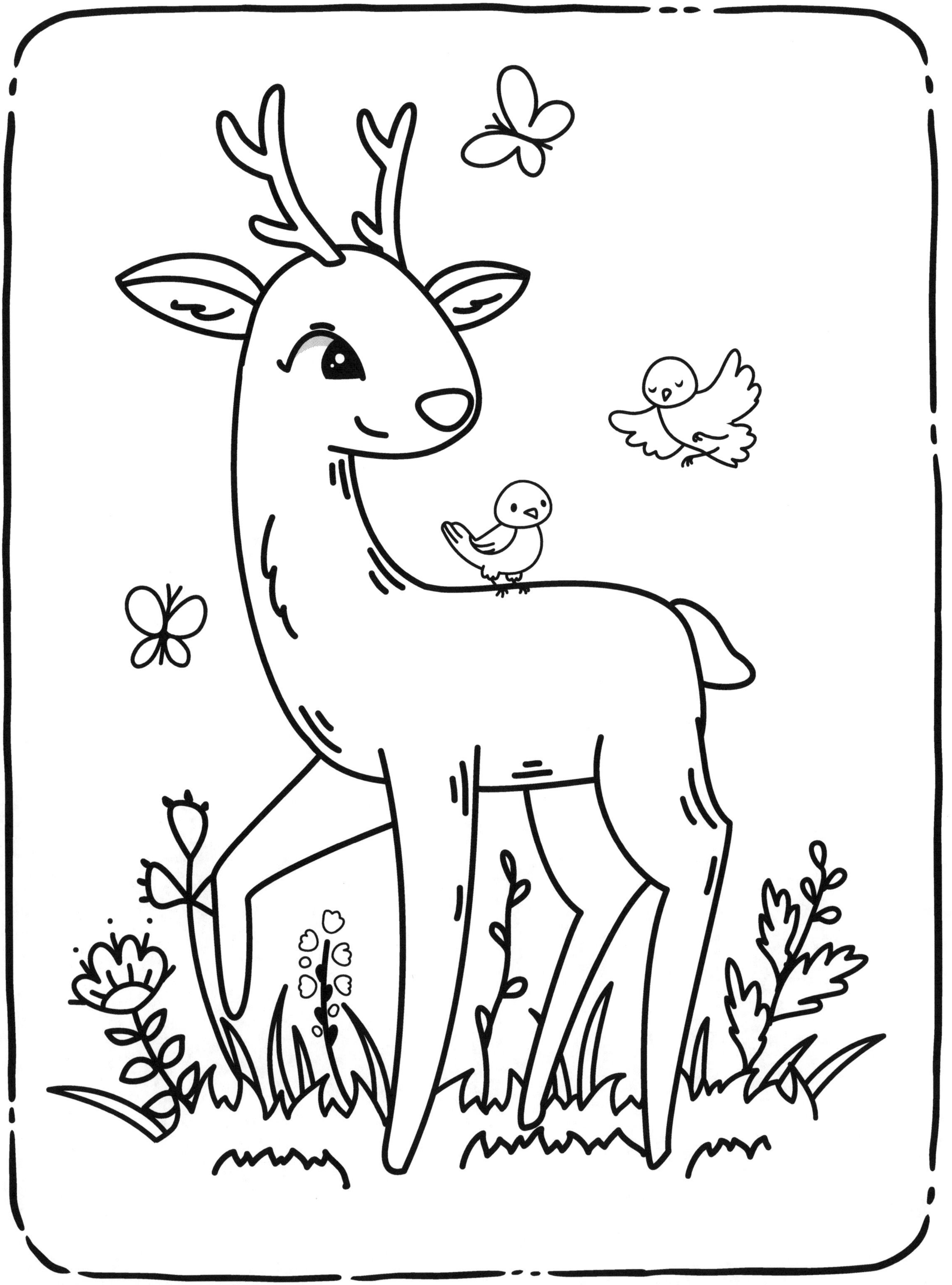

Made in the USA
Columbia, SC
14 May 2025